The Ultimate Guide To Hosting International Guests

by Alan R Gates

A comprehensive "How To" book on hosting language learners in your home. It covers a wide range of topics to help provide a positive and enriching experience for both families who host, and the learners themselves.

Copyright

ISBN: 9798867268329

Imprint: Independently published

CONTENTS

SUMMARY

In 2022, English language teaching centres in the UK taught over 225,000 full-time English language students. This is up 111% on 2021 figures and is well on the way to overcoming the downturn during the pandemic. (Source - 2023 Student Statistics Report Executive Summary, English UK, London). There are also centres of learning in Canada, USA, Australia, New Zealand, Ireland and Malta. This is a massive and growing market, and provides a huge opportunity for hosting.

It is a common practice in many countries, especially in English-speaking ones, for individuals or families to open their homes to international visitors who want to improve their language skills. Visitors may be students, their teachers, visiting lecturers, medical staff, airline staff and other professionals, and are hereafter referred to as 'guests'.

This book is a comprehensive guide to understanding the process of hosting. It covers a wide range of topics to help hosts provide a positive and enriching experience for their guests, for the host families themselves and to balance these with a more-than-decent income.

An overview of how the process typically works

Matching - Language schools or agencies often act as intermediaries, connecting host families with foreign guests. They match them with suitable host families based on preferences such as location, family composition and cultural compatibility.

Host Family Selection Interested families apply to become host families, after interviews and background checks to ensure they are suitable and can provide a safe and welcoming environment for their guests.

Accommodation - Host families provide a room (and sometimes meals) for the guest. The guest typically pays a fee to the host family, usually through the language school accommodation department for lodging and meals.

Accommodation can vary from a private room with a bathroom to a shared room with other guests.

Payment - Host families receive compensation for hosting the guest. The amount can vary depending on factors such as the location and the level of support provided - bed only, bed and evening meal or full service including breakfast and a packed lunch.

Immersive Language Learning - The primary goal of hosting is to provide the guest with an immersive English-language experience. Host families encourage their guests to speak English at home, which helps them improve their language skills rapidly.

Cultural Exchange - Hosting also promotes cultural exchange Guests get to experience daily life in the host country, including customs, traditions and activities. Host families may involve guests in family events and outings.

Support and Guidance - Host families offer support and guidance to the guests. This can include assistance with transportation, understanding local customs and helping with language practice.

Duration - The duration of the hosting experience can vary. It might range from one week to several months, depending on the guest's goals and the arrangement made between host family, the guest and the school.

Feedback and Evaluation - Language schools or agencies may regularly check in with both the host family and the guest to ensure that the experience is positive and that the language learning goals are being met.

Overall, hosting can be a very rewarding experience for both the host family and the guest, as it facilitates cultural exchange and language learning in an authentic setting.

FOREWORD

From the moment I first visited Alan and Nic, I knew they were going to be successful hosts. I could tell that the warmth and kindness they extended to me would transfer over to the students, creating a welcoming environment for their guests to feel at ease and to give them the best possible chance of settling down quickly in order to make the most of their time studying with us. After all, a student who is happy in their homestay will usually have a very positive experience all-round.

I am delighted to see such a comprehensive book written about hosting international students, as the homestay experience plays a vital part in a student's language programme. I know that it will prove to be very useful for current hosts as well as those of you thinking about stepping into this rewarding field. After many years of hosting, Alan really understands what it takes to be a successful host and I am sure that readers will find his book very informative and it will give those thinking about hosting the confidence to take the next step.

Alan and Nic – students who have stayed with you leave very positive feedback time and time again and the words they use are testament to you both … fantastic, helpful, kind, dependable, enthusiastic and friendly. Thanks for continuing to provide our students with a home away from home.

Ali Passmore, Operations Manager, ELC, Brighton, UK

PREFACE

Nic and I have been hosting English language learners in our bungalow in south-east England since 2014. In the beginning we had one spare bedroom and a shared bathroom, so we hosted one mature guest (usually over 21 years old) and long-term (3 months to 7 months duration). We provided breakfast and dinner for the guest, and this arrangement fitted in with our work and family schedules at the time, plus giving us a very useful additional source of income.

Whilst this was a good start, Nic wanted to leave her highly stressful job as a special needs teacher, so we came up with a plan to convert the bungalow, adding a top floor with two bedrooms and another bathroom. There are two single beds in one room and a double bed in the other. This permits us to host up to 4 guests at any one time, which is the legal maximum in the UK, without having to follow strict UK regulations on houses of multiple occupation (HMOs).

This has provided a better job for Nic as 'host-mother', replaced her meagre teaching salary and reduced her stress level considerably! Plus, we got our bathroom back and segregated the guest area upstairs from our area downstairs.

Since the conversion we have striven to provide the very best hosting experience to between12 and 20 guests per year and have been rewarded with many positive testimonials. We have also made many new friends, several of whom have re-visited us in later years.

Our knowledge and experience can be read in full or, if you are already a host, you can select each chapter relevant to you. In Chapter 15: Resources and Additional Tips, you will find useful website links, documents that can be amended with your own details - all of which are available as downloads and that you are welcome to print out, plus access to a free monthly newsletter 'The International Host's Chronicle - your monthly guide to hosting excellence'.

Alan Gates, September 2023.

CHAPTER 1: Choosing to Host

Understanding the Concept of Hosting

Hosting guests involves welcoming individuals from foreign countries into your home with the intention of providing them with a safe, supportive and immersive environment for learning English. It's a unique form of cultural exchange where your home becomes a bridge for international guests to experience daily life in an English-speaking environment, to introduce them to everyday spoken English and equally importantly, to provide you with a primary or secondary income.

Guests' abilities with English can vary greatly, depending on which country they come from and the level of education they obtained in their home country.

Foreign visitors may have food intolerances, food preferences, allergies to food or animals and they may be fearful of pet dogs. All these aspects must be considered, but don't be put-off by this - think how you would feel in their place.

Hosting Guests offers a Multitude of Benefits

For your guest, it's an opportunity to improve their English language skills dramatically. For you and your family, it can be a chance to learn or practice their language as well, although do bear in mind that their primary goal is for them to learn English. It also allows you to learn about and appreciate different cultures, traditions and perspectives. It is genuinely like travelling the world without leaving your home.

It can lead to lifelong friendships and connections worldwide. You might find yourself visiting your former guests in their home countries or receiving future visits from them.

Using the information in this book will help you generate extra income to cover current expenses or allow you to save for future endeavours and adventures.

Many hosts find great satisfaction in helping guests achieve their language and personal goals. Knowing you've played a role in someone's development can be incredibly rewarding and is far less complex than being their actual teacher at school.

Preparing to Become a Host Family

Before embarking on your hosting journey, it's essential to assess your suitability for this role with honesty. Here are some steps to get you started:

1. Self-Assessment - Reflect on your motivations for hosting. Are you just doing it to make as much extra money as possible? Some do and have the guests eat on their own with the cheapest foods (frozen pizzas, cheap pasta dishes and microwave ready meals). This will be a very poor experience for your guest, it may make them unhappy and then they may complain about this to the school or agency and ask to change hosts. This will not reflect well on your reputation as a quality host.

2. Cultural Sensitivity - Are you willing to adapt to accommodate your guest's cultural norms and preferences? An Islamic guest came to us from the UAE for 3 weeks, and we had to be considerate of his need for privacy and timing to pray, and to avoid any meals that contain pork, bacon or ham. That may seem obvious, but it bears repeating so as not to cause offence.

3. Family Discussion - Involve all your family members who live at home with you in the decision-making process. Hosting should be a family commitment, so ensure everyone is on board and understands the expectations. Make sure also that your children understand that a guest renting a room with you has anticipations of privacy and that they cannot enter the guest's room without being invited in by the guest and definitely not to touch any of the guest's possessions, including in the bathroom.

I am reminded of a guest who was with another host, but asked the school accommodation office to move her, because the teenage daughter of the hosts was constantly going into the guest's room and using her make-up, even though she had asked the hosts to stop the daughter invading her space. The guest was then placed with us and was able to enjoy the rest of her stay in the UK.

4. Timing - Do you have future vacations or visits already booked, and how will you handle an emergency situation like an illness or death in your family? The school can and will be flexible for you, but give these situations due consideration in advance.

5. Home Evaluation - Consider the physical aspects of your home, such as available space, sleeping arrangements and bathroom facilities. Ensure your home can reasonably accommodate a guest and most importantly that you feel comfortable with them sharing certain spaces in your home - bathroom, toilet, living room, kitchen, garden, etc. Don't forget about family pets also, which we cover in chapter 2.

6. House Rules - Establish clear rules and expectations for both your family and your guest. Do not skimp on this step and it will vastly reduce any potential issues that may arise through misunderstanding. This includes issues like curfews, meal times and both your and their responsibilities around the house. In chapter 15, you will find an example of 'House Rules' that we have adapted over the years and used successfully to communicate clear boundaries. If you change your mobile phone and get a different number or change your email address, remember to update your house rules.

7. Communication Skills - Be aware of your own communication skills, as effective communication is crucial when interacting with guests from diverse backgrounds. Be open and willing to listen and learn from your guest. Many will have only a very basic grasp of English at first, so remember to speak more slowly and clearly, facing your guest so they can pick-up that you are addressing them and not another member of your family.

If they look baffled when you speak to them, ask if they understood what you said and if not, try speaking slower and rephrasing the question or statement.

8. Financial Considerations - Hosting can provide extra income, which can be helpful for covering household expenses or saving for future goals, but be realistic and understand this is not a quick path to being a millionaire. It is an additional or maybe a sole income for you. In chapter 9 we cover financial considerations in more detail.

9. Legal and Regulatory Compliance - Familiarise yourself with any legal obligations and regulations related to hosting guests. This may include background checks, insurance, gas, electric and water tests, and other permits. We have covered the regulations pertaining to the UK in chapter 10, but be sure to check compliance for your own country and region.

Embrace Flexibility - hosting can occasionally be unpredictable, but by using this guide you will be well prepared. Be flexible and ready to adapt to different situations and needs that your guest may have.

By understanding the concept of hosting, you're setting the foundation for a rewarding and enriching experience for both your guests and your family.

CHAPTER 2: Important First Considerations

Having decided that you would like to host and before you welcome a guest into your home, there are several factors to address to ensure a smooth and enjoyable hosting experience. In this chapter, we will explore these factors, including home location and transport options, language proficiency, household pets and dietary preferences.

Location of Your Home and Transport Options

The proximity of your home to language schools or educational institutions is a critical factor for both you and your guest and the school will advise if your home is in a suitable location. A convenient location can ease transport logistics, reduce commuting time and enhance the overall experience. Consider the availability of transport, especially if they need to commute to their language school or other destinations. Familiarise yourself with public transport routes, schedules and safety precautions. If you're willing to provide transport for your guest, discuss the logistics and expectations with your hosting agency or school to ensure a smooth daily routine.

Native Language of the Host Family

While hosting, it's essential to consider your proficiency in English, especially if you plan to host guests specifically to learn the language. Native English speakers are often preferred by the schools because they provide the most authentic language immersion experience. However; non-native speakers with proficient English can also make effective hosts, as they can better understand the challenges of language acquisition and provide unique insights into the learning process.

Remember that hosting is about more than just language; it's a cultural exchange. Guests are often eager to learn about your culture and share their own, making your language proficiency just one facet of the whole experience.

Household Pets

Pets are beloved members of many households, but they can be a potential source of concern for some guests. Allergies, phobias and cultural backgrounds can influence a guest's comfort level with pets. Communicate openly with your hosting agency or school about the presence of pets in your home. This helps ensure a suitable match with a guest who is comfortable with animals. In cases where your guest is uneasy about your pets, you may need to consider temporary accommodations or arrangements.

Your personal experiences, such as guests overcoming their fear of your dog or accommodating guests with allergies to certain animals, highlight the importance of being flexible and compassionate as a host. These experiences illustrate how hosting can lead to personal growth and the breaking down of cultural barriers.

On two occasions we have had guests arrive with a fear of dogs. However, after meeting our gentle and human-loving dog, they both got over their fear very quickly. In another example we were called by the school to house two 16 year-old boys as an emergency. They had arrived from Thailand and met with their assigned host, only to discover they had 3 cats. As one of the boys was highly allergic to cats, they transferred to us for their 3 week stay.

Dietary Preferences - Carnivore, Pescatarian, Vegetarian or Vegan?

Understanding your guest's dietary preferences and restrictions is essential when planning meals. Discuss these considerations with your hosting agency or school to ensure that you can cater for your guest's culinary needs. It's vital to respect cultural and dietary differences while providing nutritious and enjoyable meals during their stay.

Sometimes, guests may not specify their dietary preferences on their application forms. As the host, you might encounter occasional surprises, but this is an opportunity to showcase your adaptability and willingness to accommodate their needs. For example, if you are a vegetarian host, you can request only vegetarian guests, or decide whether you're comfortable preparing meat or fish dishes if your guest has different dietary preferences.

By proactively addressing these important factors, you'll set the stage for a successful hosting experience. You'll contribute to creating a positive and enriching environment for language learning, cultural exchange, and, most importantly, a warm and welcoming atmosphere for your guest.

CHAPTER 3: Finding a Language School or Agency

Selecting the right language school or agency is a critical step in your journey as a host family. In this chapter, we will explore the essential factors to consider when choosing a language school or agency to partner with.

Researching Language Schools or Agencies - Their Reputation and Credibility

Before making any commitments, it's crucial to conduct thorough research to identify potential language schools or agencies. Consider factors such as their status, track record, the types of programmes they offer, payment fee scales and frequency of payment to hosts. Look for online reviews, testimonials and the school or agency's history in the industry. Do certain schools have a better educational reputation and therefore have more guests joining their courses? If so, the accommodation office will be looking for more host families and this can only be good for you.

You can also reach out to other host families and seek recommendations to help you narrow down your choices. If you know neighbours who have hosted, then have a chat with them or, even put a note in letterboxes locally asking for their impressions of language schools that they have dealt with. Don't be concerned about competition with other hosts, as most schools are desperate for new hosts and often post flyers through your letterbox.

Understanding Their Rules and Regulations

Each language school or agency will have its own set of rules and expectations for host families. These rules may cover aspects such as house rules, guest expectations and payment procedures. Take the time to review and understand these regulations to ensure you are comfortable with them and can meet their requirements.

Reading and Understanding All Written Documents

Before finalising your partnership, thoroughly read and comprehend all written documents provided by the language school or agency, including contracts, agreements and programme guidelines. Pay close attention to terms related to compensation, guest placement, and the duration of hosting. It's essential to have a clear understanding of your rights and responsibilities.

If you are in any doubt, get a family member or knowledgeable friend to read it with you to ensure your understanding.

Providing Regulatory Documents

Some language schools or agencies may require hosts to provide specific regulatory documents, such as background checks (known in the UK as DBS checks) or health and safety certifications. The vast majority of schools will require a Landlord Homeowner Gas Safety Record to cover the gas boiler, oven and hob if applicable, and any other gas appliances in your home. Some schools require an Emergency Procedures plan for Fire Safety and Evacuation. Details are provided in chapter 10 and we mention fire safety in our house rules also - see chapter 15. Ensure that you can fulfil these requirements and submit all necessary documentation in a timely manner to maintain compliance.

Establishing Lines of Communication

Establishing effective lines of communication with your chosen language school or agency is crucial for a successful hosting experience and you should have a named point of contact, usually the senior accommodation officer, and a name for whoever substitutes for them if they are otherwise engaged or on vacation.

Effective communication serves several key purposes:

Clarification - You can seek clarification on any questions or concerns you may have about the hosting process, rules, or expectations.

Emergency Situations - In case of emergencies or unexpected situations, having clear communication channels ensures that you can quickly address issues and receive support if needed.

Programme Updates - Regular updates allow you to stay informed about any changes to the guest programme. This could include details about school-organised trips or updates on hosting guidelines.

Host Get-Togethers - Some schools encourage interactions with fellow hosts and might arrange a Christmas party or a summer barbeque. We heartily recommend attending these events to pick up tips and tricks on being a better host.

Fees and Payments

Language schools and agencies may vary in the fees they offer to host families and their payment terms and schedules. While maximizing your income is essential, don't make your decision based solely on the maximum fees you can earn from a particular school or agency. Consider their overall reputation, reliability and their ability to keep you consistently supplied with guests. This has been our guiding rule and has served us well over the years.

Choosing a school or agency that is well-regarded for assigning respectful and responsible guests to hosts can lead to a more enjoyable hosting experience. Your partnership with a reputable school or agency, as discussed further in Chapter 9, will ensure a more stable and profitable hosting journey.

Most schools and agencies have a good reputation, but not all. We have worked with four different schools over the years, but generally our guests come from just two of them.

These two have good reputations for the quality of English language courses that they provide, which means they can keep us supplied with guests and with few if any 'down-periods' in between, thereby ensuring maximum profitability for us. They are also well regarded for assigning respectful guests to hosts. See further details in chapter 9 - compensation and finances.

By thoroughly researching and evaluating language schools and agencies, understanding their rules and regulations, providing necessary documents, and establishing clear lines of communication, you will be well-prepared to embark on your hosting journey with confidence.

CHAPTER 4: Preparing Your Home

Preparing your home to host international guests is a crucial step in creating a comfortable and welcoming environment. In this chapter, we will explore the essential elements of home preparation, ensuring that your guest has a pleasant and enriching stay.

Setting up a Comfortable Guest Room

Bedding - Your guest's room is their sanctuary during their stay, so it's essential to make it as welcoming as possible.. Make sure the bedding is comfortable and clean. Having a spare set of bedding and towels (flannel, hand towel and bath towel) for each room is a thoughtful touch as it ensures your guest always has fresh linens, as you may be washing or drying one set whilst the other is being used.

Storage Space - Provide adequate storage space for your guest's belongings. Clear out a portion of the closet or dresser for their use. This helps them settle in and feel more at home.

Work Space - Your school will expect a desk and chair to be provided in the room. This provides your guest with a dedicated space to work, study, or catch up on emails. Make sure there's a good Wi-Fi connection available and the password is clearly written down for them, and an adjacent power point for their laptop.

Personal Touches - Add personal touches to the room that reflect your home's personality. Consider artwork and decorations that fit in with your home's personality. It's a nice gesture that makes your guest feel valued and appreciated.

Bathroom Facilities - Shared or Separate

Bathroom Arrangements - Decide whether your guest will have access to a shared, or a separate bathroom (an ideal scenario if possible). If it's a shared bathroom, clearly communicate bathroom schedules and rules to avoid any timing conflicts. Be mindful of family members' schedules, especially if they need to get to work or school at specific times.

Cleanliness and Supplies - Ensure that the bathroom is clean, functional, and well-stocked. Regularly check and restock essential items like toilet paper, soap and clean towels. Guests should never worry about running out of these basic necessities.

Generally we have found guests bring their own toiletries, soaps and shampoos, or visit the shops the next day to buy, as some do not want the added weight of bringing items in their luggage. Previous guests will likely have left items behind, so we have a collection that we offer to new guests, if they want them.

Privacy and Safety - Make guests aware of any locks on the bathroom door and how to use them for added privacy and comfort. We have locks that can be accessed in an emergency from outside the door, as a guest locked in the bathroom is not an ideal situation!

We have heard from our guests on several occasions, of their colleagues being hosted elsewhere and being restricted to a 4 minute shower maximum and the host banging on the bathroom door to enforce this rule. Please don't be that kind of host.

Home Safety and Security

Safety Measures - Prioritise safety in your home. Regularly check and maintain smoke detectors, heat detectors and fire extinguishers to ensure they are in working order.

Emergency Procedures - Discuss emergency evacuation procedures with your guest and make sure they know where fire exits are located and any potential trip hazards. Provide a list of emergency contacts and make them feel safe and supported in your home. See further information in chapter 8.

We do not have locks on bedroom doors. This is a home and not a hotel, so we all have an expectation of trust.

House Rules and Expectations, Day and Night Timing

Establish Clear Rules - Clearly define house rules and expectations for your guest from the beginning. These rules should cover areas such as curfew, quiet hours, use of bathroom facilities and acceptable behaviour. Communicate these rules effectively to avoid misunderstandings later on.

Guest Access - Do you provide front door keys when you are not home and if they come in after you have retired to bed, which lights will you leave on for them and which should they turn off after they enter? Ensure they know the entry process.

Food or Drinks in the Bedroom - We have been strict with not allowing any food or drinks in guest rooms (other than plain water), as this will avoid any spillages that require cleaning. If you have warned them about this and a spillage occurs, then you can ask the guest to pay for specialist cleaning. There is a copy of our standard written House Rules in chapter 15 that you can download and adapt for your particular use and includes such details.

We ask them to use the dining room, if they have bought food for consumption or wish to drink a tea or coffee.

Meals, Laundry and Cleaning

Dietary Accommodations - Discuss meal times and accommodate your guest's dietary preferences and any specific meal requirements. This ensures that your guest enjoys their meals and feels at ease. Personally, we eat our main evening meal at 7pm, but this can vary on Fridays and at weekends.

Laundry and Cleaning Schedule - Define your laundry and cleaning schedule to maintain a clean and organised home throughout their stay.

Knowing what to expect helps your guest feel comfortable and prevents any potential conflicts. See chapter 7 for full details.

Disposal of Rubbish and Recycling

Waste Separation - Explain your household's rubbish disposal (including sanitary towels) and recycling procedures to your guest. Provide clear instructions on how to separate and dispose of waste responsibly.

In several countries it is common practice not to flush used toilet paper, but clarify that this is acceptable and expected in the UK.

Advise them that any blockage of drains, damage to items and services within the home and any operational concerns, must be made to you promptly, so that issues can be addressed and prevent them from becoming more significant problems.

Mobile Phone Use

Establish guidelines for mobile or cell phone use, especially at the dinner table. Encourage face-to-face communication during meals to facilitate language practice and cultural exchange. There may be appropriate times for them to use their phones to access a translation app, if they are struggling with how to say something in English, or to show you photos of their home, family, and trips they have been on. Ensure that both you and your guest understand and respect these guidelines by setting the correct example yourself.

Our younger guests have, on occasion, been scrolling through their mobile phones at the dinner table, which was not acceptable to us and required recommunicating.

Think of preparing your guest accommodation for what you would expect to find if the roles were reversed and you were the guest, and it will set the foundation for a successful hosting experience. It ensures that your guest feels comfortable, safe and welcome in your home. Additionally, it helps to prevent potential misunderstandings and conflicts by establishing a framework for daily life during their stay.

CHAPTER 5: Matching with a Guest

The process of matching with a suitable guest is a crucial step in hosting foreign language learners. In this chapter, we will explore the various aspects of matching with a guest, considering factors such as age, hosting duration, lifestyle preferences and communication with your language school or agency. All schools should send a representative to see your home and the accommodation that you offer, and many write up your basic details (family members, age, work and interests), so that potential guests also have a choice of who they stay with.

Mature Guests vs. Under 18's - Pros and Cons

Decide whether you are open to hosting mature guests (adults) or those under 18 years-old. Each group comes with its own set of challenges and rewards. Mature guests may offer more respect, independence and conversational depth, whilst under 18's may require more supervision but can bring youthful energy and enthusiasm. We have had both over the years - most of the under 18's have been respectful and considerate, but a couple have evidently still been 'children' and required closer supervision and a certain amount of control. In the absence of their own parents back home you effectively become their 'parents' for the duration of their stay.

With under 18's you have an elevated level of responsibility, including escorting them from their first arrival. You may be required to pick them up either from the airport or from the school, or maybe the school has organised a bus or taxi for them, and to deliver them back to the school or airport on their departure. Usually they make their own way to school during their courses, but always check arrangements and ensure you are compensated accordingly for the transport costs. With one guest we were expected to absorb the cost of a taxi on arrival, without compensation. See details in 'Always Read the School's Small-Print'.

Short-Term vs. Long-Term Hosting Duration

Determine your preference for short-term or long-term hosting. Short-term hosting (one week to three weeks) may be more

flexible and less demanding, while long-term hosting (one month to seven months, or more) can provide a more stable and extended cultural exchange experience. Getting to know the longer-term guests has been much more rewarding for us personally and often led to life-long friendships and offers to meet and stay with them if visiting their home countries in the future. We are still in close contact with ex-guests from Korea, Japan, Switzerland, France, Colombia, Brazil and Kazakhstan.

Cooking or Allowing Guests to Cook

Discuss cooking arrangements with the school. Decide whether you will provide meals for guests or allow them to cook in your kitchen. This choice may depend on your guest's culinary skills, dietary preferences and having a spare cupboard in your kitchen to allow storage of the guests ingredients. This choice will probably have been part of the schools host-selection process anyway. Bear in mind that should there be a kitchen emergency, whether you are present or not, it may negate your household insurance, again - check the small-print of your insurance schedule. We have always opted to cook, as we have a small kitchen and it avoids potential accidents and the associated liabilities. See further details in chapter 7.

Smoking or Non-Smoking

Clarify your household's smoking policy and communicate it to the school and your guest. Determine whether you are comfortable hosting a smoker and if you have designated smoking areas on your property. We say in our House Rules (see chapter 15), that we are a non-smoking home, but that guests are free to smoke in the garden with an ashtray provided by us.

The Matching Process

The matching process involves your language school or agency selecting a guest who aligns with your preferences and household dynamics. Be prepared to provide extra information about your family, home environment and any specific hosting conditions you may have. If they have done their job correctly, you will have confirmation of the guest's name, age, home country, flight arrival details, any allergies and duration of stay. Armed with this information you are now well informed and ready to welcome your guest.

Communicating with the School or Agency

Schools and agencies usually have a policy whereby if you host a guest who is incompatible, or the guest is uncomfortable in some way with you, then each party has a one-week notice period to change guest or hosts. This is rare, but it does happen occasionally and is nothing to worry about. Just maintain a professional attitude, treat guests with respect and contact the accommodation officer. One guest thought that our boiler was turned off at night so she couldn't get a hot shower and asked to change host family. Although we showed her that she had turned the temperature control on the shower to cold, she still wasn't happy, so we agreed to part ways. See also chapter 13.

Always Read the School's Small-Print

Review all agreements and contracts carefully, paying attention to the finer details. Understand the terms and conditions set by your language school or agency, including any financial obligations, cancellation policies and dispute resolution procedures.

As a valid example, when we accepted a guest from a new school, we discovered in their small-print that we were expected to transport the guest on first arrival and on departure from the school to our home and vice-versa, bearing the associated costs or pay for a taxi.

As the taxi fare (both ways) amounted to 19% of the weekly fee, we were unhappy with that arrangement and refused future guests from that school.

Matching with the right guest is essential for a harmonious hosting experience. Aligning your hosting preferences with your guest's expectations ensures that both parties have a positive and fulfilling experience. Effective communication with your language school or agency is crucial to facilitate this matching process.

CHAPTER 6: Welcoming Your Guest

Welcoming your guest into your home is a pivotal moment in your hosting journey. In this chapter, we will explore the key aspects of this process, ensuring a smooth transition for both you and your guest.

Meeting Your Prospective Guest

Meeting your prospective guest is an exciting opportunity to get to know each other. From your perspective, it's a chance to assess compatibility and address any initial concerns. From their perspective, it's an introduction to their host family and living environment.

The Arrival Process

Plan the arrival process. Coordinate transportation arrangements if that is part of the school's requirements that you have agreed to, such as picking up your guest from the airport or bus station, and ensure that their journey to your home is as comfortable as possible.

Bear in mind three things - First, they will often be very tired and probably stressed from their long journey. For example, a flight from Japan is 4 hours to Hong Kong, probably with a stop-over of several hours, then a long-haul flight of 13 hours to Heathrow, followed by train, bus or taxi ride to your home, which can easily add up to 24 hours or more. Second, many guests are not well travelled and may have never left their home country ever before, so will naturally be anxious. Third, English is not their native language, and combined with the first two points will result in them being a little shell-shocked.

First Impressions and Making Your Guest Feel Welcome

Create a warm and inviting atmosphere to make your guest feel welcome from the moment they step into your home. Small gestures, such as smiling, speaking slowly and clearly, offering them a drink of tea, coffee or water, can go a long way in building a positive first impression.

Initial Orientation and Introductions

Provide an initial orientation to your home, including key areas like their bedroom, bathroom and communal spaces. Introduce your guest to other family members. If it is late in the evening, tell them that they'll meet other family members the next day (thinking of children or maybe grandparents already in bed at this time).

Clearly Explain Your House Rules and Encourage Questions

Show them your written house rules and ask them to read them when they feel ready, emphasizing the importance of clear communication. Have a copy of the rules to refer to at breakfast time, in case they have any questions.

Lighting, Heating and Fresh Air

Ensure that your guest is comfortable with the lighting, heating and ventilation in their room. Explain how to adjust these amenities to suit their preferences - thermostatic radiator valves spring to mind, which windows can be opened, etc.

Electrical Appliances, Voltage, Adapters and WiFi Connectivity

Familiarise your guest with the electrical outlets in their room and have one spare multi-adapter for them. Inform them about the local voltage (220 – 240v in the UK) and advise them where they can buy further adapters if they need them.

Don't worry about them taking adapters with them when they leave. We have found many more left in our rooms, so have ended up with quite a collection for future guests!

You will see in our House Rules (see chapter 15) we state the WiFi connection name and the password for them to use.

Generally speaking, we leave the following 4 points to the day after their arrival, so as not to overwhelm them - remember they may be jet-lagged from their journey.

Downloading a Weather App

The weather in the UK can be unpredictable, so suggest that your guest download a weather app onto their phones to check daily forecasts, preferably every morning before leaving home. This can help them prepare for any weather changes with appropriate clothing. Remind them that the UK is an island and changeable weather is completely normal here - '4 seasons in one day' is a common expression and rain can appear within a few minutes of sunshine.

Map and Directions To and From the School

Provide detailed directions to your guest's school or language centre, including bus numbers and schedules if available, or at least a web address to the local bus company so they can research bus routes and timetables for themselves. We have annually updated printouts with a basic map showing bus stops and bus numbers. Remind them that buses go in both directions, so be careful to cross the street for a return bus after they leave school.

We often have new guests when another guest is also still with us. If both guests are attending the same school, we ask the old guest to escort the new guest to school on the first day of their course, which all have been happy to do.

Local Wildlife

If your area has local wildlife, educate your guest about it. Share information about any animals they might encounter and safety precautions to take when outdoors. For us this is urban foxes roaming evenings and nights. We are on the border of three fox families' territory, so often see up to seven foxes, posturing and 'shouting' at and to each other in the middle of the street. Although they can sound fierce, they are wary of human contact so will keep a safe distance from people and are not a danger in any way.

Meeting Your Friends and Joining in with Family Events

Include your guest in family events and gatherings if at all possible. Introduce them to your friends, creating further opportunities for social interaction and cultural exchange. We and two sets of neighbours meet up every Friday after working hours to share a few snacks, have a few drinks and generally to have a chat for an hour or so. That has proved an opportune time to introduce guests to friends and they have been supportive and happy to talk to our guests, thereby enhancing their learning experience.

CHAPTER 7: Meals, Laundry and Cleaning

Efficiently preparing meals, doing the laundry and other household processes are important to maximise your profit, without diluting the hosting experience for your guest. This is probably the most important information on hosting and we wish we had known these tips and tricks prior to our first hosting all those years ago!

Cooking for Your Guest

Preparing meals for your guest can be a delightful cultural exchange experience. However, please take note of any food allergies, dislikes, cultural preferences or religious bans that the school has informed you of, prior to the guest arrival. However, be aware that guests may not have noted allergies, etc. on their application to the school or agency This is not uncommon.

For example; Muslims do not drink alcohol and do not eat any pork or pork products - bacon, sausages, lardons, pancetta, etc. so be careful not to include any such ingredients. We have also had several guests who didn't eat certain vegetables, didn't like garlic or chilli spices (or any vegetables at all, in one case!). However; knowing the importance of eating fresh vegetables, Nic has often liquidised onions, mushrooms and other veg into the gravy or sauce, so as not to degrade the flavour for the others who are eating the same dish. Of course, do not use any ingredients to which the guest has a known allergy.

You should have already covered the carnivore, pescatarian, vegetarian and vegan choices as noted in chapter 2, under the heading Dietary Preferences. Some schools request you to provide a takeaway lunch for the guest, for which you will be provided additional compensation (check this in your agreement with the school). As a standard, we provide a sandwich or roll - ham, cheese, salad, etc., a packet of crisps, a piece of fresh fruit, all in a sealed plastic bag and a small bottle of water.

Meal Times and What to Serve

We make it clear in our house rules (see chapter 15), that breakfast is served between 7am to 8am on school days, and 7am to 9am on weekends and we are strict about this, as we do have our own lives to lead after all. Dinner is at 7pm during school days and may vary on Friday evening and at weekends, depending on family arrangements, but we always let the guests know the day before on this timing.

Be consistent with your meal times if at all possible, as it definitely makes planning easier for you and also for your guest. If your guest may be going out after school, ask them to text or call you at least 4 hours before the meal whether they are going to be present, as wasted food is lost profit for you. If they are going on out-of-school trips or have a flight to catch, be prepared for flexibility to accommodate such situations.

It is common for guests to team-up with new friends from the school and have an evening meal out, maybe once or twice a week. We encourage outside trips to expand their horizons, and it saves you cooking for them occasionally.

Our breakfast standard is a choice of 2 cereals, with milk in a small jug (to minimise waste), a small glass of orange or apple juice and tea or coffee of their choice, 1 slice of toast with butter and jam or marmalade, and a small fruit yoghurt pot. We do not supply a cooked breakfast, as this will 'eat-in' (pun intended) to your profit.

If you are used to serving main meals at the dinner table, we strongly recommend not doing so with your guests. Instead, serve the meals onto plates in your kitchen and take them into the dining room. This gives you full control over portion sizes, as we have found that some guests helping themselves can, on occasion, leave little for other family members.

We also only provide fresh water with all meals, but we chill 2 bottles of water in the fridge overnight, which adds to the impression of freshness and is a bonus in hot weather.

Never offer guests beer, wine, etc. as that will set a precedent and severely cut your profit margin. We tell adults that if they want to buy alcohol for themselves that is okay, and we can keep it in the fridge for them. This of course depends on your available fridge space.

If a guest is studying at home, we are happy for them to make an extra tea or coffee, but to let us know before they use the kettle, in case of accidental spillage. Regarding coffee making, we have a bean-to-cup machine for ourselves, but have a good quality instant coffee available for guests.

Plan your meals, preferably a minimum of one week in advance. This allows you to be selective during your weekly shopping trips and not to overbuy or underbuy quantities. Remember to source supermarket own brands that have a good flavour, rather than more expensive big name brands. There are many useful reviews online of supermarket brand products that are as good as, if not better than, named brands. This will reduce waste and therefore greatly help your profits.

Most hosts do all the clearing up, but as part of the learning process, we assign small jobs to guests - getting a bottle of chilled water from the fridge, clearing and stacking the plates, etc. We don't expect or ask them to do the washing-up as that is part of our job as hosts, but it all helps them to feel included and part of the family. We have found many naturally offer to help anyway.

One amusing anecdote here - we find that many guests like to take a photograph of their meals before eating as an aide-memoire of their visit, especially if they are trying a new dish with flavours that they don't normally get in their home countries. So don't be alarmed by this, think of it as a compliment to your culinary skills!

Laundry

Establish clear laundry practices and schedules to ensure that your guest can manage their clothing and personal items.

Most school protocols say one wash per week of clothes, for which we supply a particular size of laundry bag to each guest.

In the early days we had big laundry bags that had a tendency to stretch and guests took advantage of that to cram in as much as they possibly could. Now we have more rigid and smaller bags and we make it clear to them that it is one wash only, so they are not to mix colours. Any colour bleed to lighter colour clothes are the responsibility of the guests, so long as you have made them aware of that fact. However; we do use Dylon Colour-Catcher sheets in each wash, just in case.

A valuable lesson that we learned early on, is that some guests (particularly those under 18 years old) are used to mum doing their washing without question and often every day, so they have no qualms about changing t-shirts twice a day and having a fresh pair of trousers or jogging pants on every day, even though yesterday's pair are perfectly fine. In these cases, spray fresheners like Febreze are your best friend. If the garment doesn't smell or look dirty, pull it into shape, give it a spray of freshener, let it dry completely, then fold neatly and put in in with the other laundered garments.

Excess use of washing detergent and conditioner are one of those 'hidden' costs that you need to be aware of and minimise.

Cleaning

If you have guests either sharing rooms or sharing a bathroom, make it clear in your house rules that this is not a hotel - see chapter 15. It is your home and, for the duration of their stay it is their home, so they should leave the bathroom in a clean and tidy state for the next person using it. Generally, we do a quick dust and vacuum every Monday when the guest is at school. We also include a clean out of the shower drain, as soap residues and long hair can lead to potential blockages. There should not be a need to do any deep cleaning, as we save that for guest handover day.

Change the bedding and towels, if that is your agreed process. We also use the time to check furniture, paintwork, appliances and electrical cables/connections for wear and tear, so that any issues can be swiftly remedied. A glance or light touch is usually enough, but it is at your own discretion.

Tidiness is the guest's own responsibility, we just lift items off the floor for ease of vacuuming.

Your efficiency in organising these procedures by repetition will quickly become second-nature to you and will make your life much easier, plus it will give the guest confidence that you know what you are doing and are in full control, after all, who doesn't like a clean room?

One small tip - make a checklist of things to do and tick them off as you do them.

CHAPTER 8: Safety and Well-Being

Ensuring the safety and well-being of your guest is a top priority when hosting.
In this chapter, we will explore various aspects of safety and well-being to help you create a secure and supportive environment for your guest.

Ensuring the Safety of Your Guest

Provide guidance on how they can stay safe both inside and outside your home. Share safety tips, such as closing doors for privacy or to stop a friendly pet wandering into their space, putting personal belongings out of sight in a drawer and being aware of trip hazards, possibly going into your garden or on stairs for example.

At the bottom and the top of our stairs we have night lights in nearby sockets, that come on automatically when main hall lights are turned off. This allows for a low-level illumination when using the bathroom at night and when returning late in the evening after the family has retired to bed.

Travelling After Sunset

Discuss the safety considerations of travelling after sunset. Advise your guest on the availability of public transport, well-lit or badly-lit routes and any precautions they should take when venturing out at night. Obviously this applies to certain towns and cities and maybe in specific areas of your town, rather than where your home is located.

We have a large park nearby which is an excellent short-cut between schools and home, but is poorly lit at night with many patches of bushes. That is not to say it is dangerous, but we advise guests to be sensibly aware and stick to well-lit roads.

Access to the House

As you can see on our House Rules (further details in chapter 15), if guests are out after 9pm, then we provide a front door key and procedure when entering the house, informing them to lock the door behind them, put the key in a bowl (or a key hook if you have it) so that with a quick glance we can see if they have returned, turn off the outside light, again so that we know with a glance that they are back home safely. We also emphasise that they be as quiet as possible.

As an aside, we ask guests to leave outdoor shoes near the exit door and swap to slippers or flip-flops for access to bedrooms and communal rooms. This helps to avoid potential cleaning issues.

Alcohol and Drug Use Locally, and Expected Consequences

Inform your guest about local laws and regulations related to alcohol and drug use. Advise them to be aware of and avoid possible drunks in the town, especially at weekends.

Evenings out with fellow students or friends are much to be desired as "safety in numbers".

Pick-pocketing and Scams

It is sad to say, but incidences of pick-pocketing seem to be increasing each year. Educate your guest about common pick-pocketing techniques, scams and confidence tricks, in person and on-line, that may occur in your area and when they are visiting other cities and tourist attractions. Tell guests to keep shoulder bags and backpacks on the front and never put mobile phones, wallets or credit cards in their back pockets, and to be aware who is nearby when they are at an ATM.

One female guest was robbed while attempting to buy a train ticket from a machine. A man approached and advised her that cash was required, indicating an ATM machine nearby.

After she had withdrawn £350, the man grabbed the cash and ran away. A painful lesson well-learned.

Health and Medications

Encourage your guest to maintain a healthy lifestyle, get regular exercise and manage stress. If your guest takes any medications, ensure they have an adequate supply and understand how to access medical assistance if needed. The school is usually the first port of call for medical matters, but if it is after hours then NHS 111 can help. If you think medical help is needed swiftly, use 111 online, in the NHS app or call 111 from a mobile phone. NHS contact details are shown in chapter 15.

We had a guest who had not informed the school of his ADHD and daily medications, which we discovered within hours of his arrival. It turned out that without his medication it could be potentially concerning and we had to speak with him in a more gentle way, so as not to be the trigger for his condition. He had brought his medications with him, so there was no crisis event during his stay with us - it was just a question of being informed, and as Nic was a special needs teacher, her knowledge on how to deal with potential situations proved invaluable.

Do not give guests any of your own medications, not even paracetamol, as you have no idea of their medical history or any contraindications of medicines that they are or have recently been taking. This has never happened to us in ten years, so do not be overly concerned with this point. If a guest is ill and confined to their bedroom, make sure to contact the school and take their advice on providing additional meals and support, also check any financial compensation to cover this.

A mature female guest from Finland who came for a 2 week stay, contracted a stomach infection and spent twelve out of fourteen days in the house with us. We informed her of the nearest A&E hospital and gave her a bottle of water to take for the long wait at the department.

Back home, we provided unlimited supplies of hot drinks for her and checked on her every few hours until she recovered. Needless to say, she was very grateful and we are still in contact with her after many years.

Emergency Procedures and Contacts

The school should always be the first point of contact in all cases. Each school should provide you with an out-of-hours number, however; it pays to outline emergency procedures for your guest, including whom to contact in case of medical emergencies, accidents, or other urgent situations. Provide a list of essential contacts, such as local hospitals, NHS 111 service, local walk-in clinics and your own contact information. This can all be included on your house rules document (see details in chapter 15) and only remind your guest verbally, if and when such a situation occurs.

Prioritising safety and well-being will ensure that your guest feels secure and supported during their stay. By addressing potential risks and providing guidance, you empower them to make informed decisions and respond to their new environment confidently. See also chapter 10 on legal and regulatory considerations.

CHAPTER 9: Compensation and Finances

Managing finances is an essential aspect of hosting foreign language guests, and it's crucial to have a clear understanding of your financial expectations and responsibilities.

Your Financial Expectations

Establish clear financial expectations from the outset. Discuss payment arrangements, any fees associated with hosting and the method and schedule of payments with your hosting agency or school. Ensure both parties have a shared understanding of financial obligations. The main school we have been with pays directly into our business banking account weekly every Wednesday morning and has never missed a payment. Another school we use pays every two weeks, so arrangements do vary and you need to manage your budget accordingly. Remember you are expending money by purchasing food, cleaning materials, and insurance premiums in advance, a proportion of which can be offset against the school fees received.

As a typical example - For a single guest in one bedroom with a shared bathroom, we are paid (prices correct in 2023) £165.00 per week to cover bed, breakfast and evening meal. For guests requiring a packed lunch, we are paid an extra £5.00 per day. So, if like us, you have two bedrooms with a guest in each, then you can expect £1320.00+ per month income. Bear in mind that each school has different rates and may have a high-season and a low-season variation of these amounts. Both our main schools have historically increased their payments once per year to help cover inflation and other added costs incurred.

If guests go travelling and are away from your home for a week or so, then generally schools will pay 50% of the normal weekly fee, as a retention.

Food and material costs have averaged out to about £50.00 per guest per week, but we have improved our margins by bulk-buying of staple foods, such as pasta, rice, potatoes and also of cleaning materials, such as laundry detergent, washing up liquid, etc., so it is possible to reduce this overall to about £35.00 per guest per week.

We also grow some vegetables in our garden, which is a useful supplement, but may not be possible for you, depending on garden space, time available or inclination to green-fingers.

Visible and Hidden Costs

Identify both visible and hidden costs associated with hosting

Visible costs may include direct expenses related to accommodating your guest - food is the most obvious, detergent and fabric conditioner for the laundry, cleaning materials for the bedroom and bathroom.

Hidden costs can encompass additional utilities and other incidental expenses that sometimes are forgotten. For example, water rates - often greater than you may have thought, due to more people having a shower every day rather than the usual two and double the toilet flushing, plus extra use of electricity and gas.

Insurance is often overlooked as well. Be sure to ask the school what their insurance covers regarding accidental damage caused by your guest (but don't necessarily expect this to be their responsibility). See chapter 10 section on liability and insurance for further details.

Understanding the full financial picture can help you budget much more effectively and ensure you make decent margins and therefore a healthy profit.

Hosting Fees and Payments Received

It is vital to keep accurate records of hosting payments received, not just for you, but also for any financial accountants and tax authorities. Plus it makes it easier for you to work out exactly how much profit you are making.

Tax Implications of Keeping Good Records

Understand the tax implications of hosting foreign language guests in your region or country. Maintain accurate records of income and expenses related to hosting, as these records may be required for tax reporting purposes. Consult with a tax professional or advisor for guidance on tax compliance.

In the UK we are allowed (currently in 2023) to earn £7,500 per year from renting out rooms, before having to pay any tax, however; a proportion of gas, water, electricity, food, drink, cleaning materials, etc. can be offset as expenses against this amount. Further details are available through HMRC in the UK and a link is provided in chapter 15.

Managing Financial Arrangements

Establish clear communication channels for financial matters. Discuss payment methods, deadlines and any necessary arrangements for handling money transfers. A separate bank account just for hosting makes life much easier for you and for your accountant. Maintain open and transparent communication with your hosting agency or school regarding any financial concerns or questions.

Occasionally guests may receive parcels from home. When a parcel arrives in the UK, one parcel in every thousand (guesstimate) may be subject to assessment by the postal service/HMRC and if so, will be subject to a taxation fee and a handling charge, depending on parcel contents and value stated on the label. Without this payment being made in advance, the parcel will not be delivered, so please advise your guest of this fact.

On two occasions guests have asked us to buy items from Amazon for them and have given their credit card details to make the payment.

This caused major issues as Amazon thought we were making a purchase with a stolen credit card and froze our account.

The way around this situation is for the guest to give you cash, and you buy the item with your card in your name. Alternatively, politely refuse to buy on their behalf, to avoid this situation completely.

Guest Difficulty with Payments or Loss of Money

In cases where your guest encounters financial difficulties or experiences loss of money, approach the situation with empathy and open communication. Generally speaking this is not your responsibility and the school should be able to arrange a temporary loan for their students and they should always be the first point of contact in these circumstances. If you wish to help, discuss potential solutions with the school, such as adjusting payment schedules or helping your guest find appropriate resources for financial assistance.

Clear financial arrangements and responsible management of finances are essential for a successful hosting experience and a healthy profit. By addressing financial expectations, tracking costs, maintaining records, and handling financial challenges with sensitivity, you can ensure that both you and your guests have a positive experience throughout the hosting period.

CHAPTER 10: Legal and Regulatory Considerations

Legal Obligations and Responsibilities for a Safe and Compliant Hosting Environment.

Immigration and Visa Compliance

You should not need to familiarise yourself with the legal obligations and responsibilities related to hosting foreign guests in your region, as this should have been dealt with by the school and the agency in the guests home country.

The accommodation department may contact you a few weeks before the guest is due, if they have any issues with receiving their visas to enter the UK. This has happened to us a few times, but the school always gave us the option of an alternative guest in these circumstances.

Housing Regulations

Depending on your location, there may be housing regulations, such as Houses of Multiple Occupation (HMO) regulations – UK rules, that you need to comply with when hosting multiple guests. Ensure that your home meets these requirements and that you have the necessary permits, licenses or certifications.

In our situation, we only had to ensure a connected series of mains powered heat/smoke detectors, upstairs and down, and a basic set of rules for evacuation in case the detectors were triggered. Again, the school will advise on the level of detection and procedures necessary, so don't overly worry about this point, but run through a potential scenario in your mind so that you are ready, if such information is requested or if an emergency genuinely occurs (hopefully never).

Specific Requirements from Hosting Agencies or Schools

Hosting agencies or schools may have specific requirements or guidelines for hosts. It is essential to understand and follow these to maintain a good working relationship.

These requirements may pertain to accommodation standards, safety measures, or any other aspects of hosting.

Personal Liability and Insurance Coverage

Contact your insurance provider to discuss your liability and insurance coverage as a host. Ensure that you are adequately covered for hosting guests. Consider whether you need additional coverage for incidents that may occur during a guest's stay and clarify what is covered and what is not. Hopefully you never have to use the insurance, but don't expose yourself by not having coverage in place. A claim by a guest could negate all your profits in one step, or worse.

Thankfully in 10 years, we haven't needed to use our insurance (famous last words!), but better safe than sorry.

School or Agency Insurance

Understand the extent of insurance coverage provided by the hosting agency or school. While some may offer coverage for minor breakages or damages caused by the guest, don't assume this is the case for all agencies. Always check with the school or agency regarding their policies. This helps in avoiding misunderstandings and ensures that you are financially protected.

Regulations for Hosting Guests Under 18 Years Old

If you plan to host students under 18 years old, be aware of any special regulations and safeguards that may apply. These regulations are in place to ensure the safety and well-being of minors. It's crucial to follow them diligently.

Background Checks

In some regions, background checks, such as the Disclosure and Barring Service (DBS) check in the UK, may be required for hosting minors. Ensure you have the necessary background checks in place and are in compliance with such requirements.

More information on obtaining DBS checks is available in chapter 15 and be aware these can take from a few days to several weeks, so get your application sent out well in advance.

Parental Consent and Supervision

Hosting agencies or schools should handle parental consent forms and additional supervision requirements for minors. However, always verify this with the school to ensure that all necessary precautions are taken to protect the guests under 18. Many such guests arrive in a school group with their teachers, who take ultimate responsibility for them.

Curfew and Communication

Schools often have curfew times for guests under 18. Ensure that both you and your guest are aware of these times. Clear communication is essential in this regard. If a minor guest is going to miss their curfew due to exceptional circumstances, insist that they call or text you, and have an emergency contact phone number in case of any unforeseen situations. Open and accurate communication is key to ensuring the safety and well-being of the young guests under your care.

In summary, compliance with legal and regulatory requirements is crucial for hosting any guests. Understanding your legal obligations, ensuring proper insurance coverage, and following any specific regulations for hosting minors are vital steps to create a secure and compliant hosting environment. By taking these measures, you not only protect yourself but also provide a safe and comfortable experience for your guests, fostering a positive hosting relationship.

CHAPTER 11: Language Learning Strategies

Total immersion in a foreign language in an unfamiliar country is daunting at best. Whilst the school is obviously the primary source of their English language learning, even as a host you also have an important and useful role to play.

Creating an English Language-Friendly Environment

Encourage your guest in an English language-friendly environment. Advise the use of English in all daily conversations, both within and outside the home. Provide language resources such as books and magazines in English for their use in your home. Maybe share a TV or film night with them occasionally and ask if it would help them to have English subtitles on.

We have avoided having TVs in guest bedrooms, as that could undermine learning strategies if they tune-in to their own language programmes or use subtitles. However; we do have the aerial connections necessary in place for the future, if required.

Encouraging Language Practice

Promote active language practice by engaging your guest in conversations and discussions. Encourage them to express their thoughts and opinions, even if their language skills are still developing. Create a supportive atmosphere where they feel comfortable speaking in English. Do not be too quick to say the words for them, be patient with them and let them strive to remember their lessons and the words to convey what they want to say. After they have tried, correct their use of words, phrases and context.

Chatting with the Students During and After Meal Times

Meal times are ideal opportunities for language practice. Engage in conversations with your guest during meals, sharing stories, discussing different foods and customs.

Encourage post-meal discussions to reinforce language skills and create a relaxed atmosphere for communication.

Ask them how their lessons went at school, what aspect of English they studied, and ask for examples of the subject matter. We also have fun explaining colloquial English, slang words and phrases, and regional accents to them.

By the way - did you know that cows in the UK moo in regional accents! No joke - google it for yourselves.

Many times we have chatted with our guests well into the evening and have learnt so much ourselves from this cultural exchange. We have also seen and heard how their understanding and use of English has blossomed, and their confidence with speaking English.

Verbal and Non-Verbal Communication

Help your guest understand not only the words, but also the nuances of verbal and non-verbal communication. Explain cultural differences in body language, tone of voice and gestures, and encourage your guest to observe and adapt to these cues. You will find that some guests occasionally have difficulty pronouncing certain letters and combinations of the English alphabet.

English can be a difficult language with, for example, different pronunciations of "though, through, rough, cough," etc. Be patient with their efforts and gently correct them whenever possible - they will thank you for it. In chapter 15 you will find a document titled 'English Is A Funny Language' - print this out for your guests to have fun with!

As Nic and I are ex-teachers, we correct guests where they have made mistakes and they are always grateful for the extra lesson, as it all goes towards their greater understanding of English.

Using Teaching Materials and Resources (Optional)

While formal teaching materials are not required from hosts, some may choose to incorporate them into the hosting experience. You can explore language learning apps, textbooks and online resources, if both you and your guest find them beneficial. Ensure that their use aligns with your guest's goals and preferences, and doesn't go against the schools' language goals.

You can also put a few magazines or maybe a current newspaper in the guest bedrooms, for less formal encouragement.

Supporting your guest's language learning journey enhances their overall experience and contributes to their language proficiency. Creating a language-friendly environment, encouraging practice and using teaching materials (if desired) help your guest gain confidence and fluency in English.

CHAPTER 12: Activities, Visits and Clubs

Cultural Activities, Places to Visit and Outings

School Programmes - Language schools often have a wide range of programmes and activities for their students. These programmes can include induction days, guided tours of the local town and landmarks, and even longer trips to famous destinations. The school will give them print-outs every week of guided tours via coach with other students, to places like Stonehenge, Bath, Oxford, Cambridge, Windsor Castle and many more UK locations. Ensure that your guest is aware of the school's programme offerings and encourages their participation.

Weekend Trips - Encourage your guests to explore during weekends or free time. One guest of ours, a lady from Kazakhstan, was away every single weekend of her stay, to Dublin, Edinburgh, Paris, Lisbon, Prague and other European and UK destinations

This fosters immense confidence in those who have never left their home country before, to be truly independent and also gives you family time, to do your own things, to draw a breath and to assess how you are doing on your hosting journey.

Cultural Activities - Recommend visits to museums (free of charge in the UK), historical sites, festivals and cultural performances. These activities allow your guest to immerse themselves in the local culture and gain a deeper understanding of the region.

Local Tourism Resources - Whenever you're out and about, visit the local tourist office and collect a selection of brochures or information about local attractions. You will also often find these brochures in the entrances of pubs that you may be visiting for lunch. Leave these on the bedroom desks for your guests to peruse. It's a thoughtful touch that helps your guests discover additional places to visit.

Local Sports Facilities, Gyms, and Clubs

Physical Activities - Share information about local sports facilities, gyms, and clubs with your guest. This helps them stay active, maintain their well-being, and engage with the local community. Encourage them to explore physical activities that interest them.

Connecting with Locals - Suggest that your guests participate in sports or hobbies popular in your area. This can be an excellent way for them to meet and interact with locals, fostering cultural exchange and creating opportunities for international friendships.

One Colombian guest joined a local kick-about football game with people he had never met before and went every week during his 6 month stay. We went along a couple of times to support him and cheered him on from the sidelines!.

Attending Local Sports Events - If there are local sports events in your area, inform your guests about them. For sports enthusiasts, attending a local football match, basketball game, or other sporting events can be an exciting and memorable experience.

Several of our guests both male and female, have been football fans and so they were excited to be able to visit our local team - Brighton and Hove Albion. One was here after his schooling on a two-year work visa and so purchased a season ticket to the Amex Stadium for the Premier League season.

Cultural exchange is a powerful tool for promoting empathy, cultural awareness, and international friendships. It enriches the hosting experience by providing both hosts and guests with opportunities to learn, share, and grow together. By encouraging your guests to engage in cultural activities, visit local landmarks and participate in local sports or clubs, you contribute to their holistic cultural immersion and help create unforgettable memories during their stay.

CHAPTER 13: Navigating Challenges

Hosting can be a rewarding experience, but it may also come with its share of challenges. In this chapter, we will explore common challenges and effective strategies to overcome them, ensuring a positive hosting experience for both you and your guest.

Common Challenges and How to Overcome Them

Identify common challenges that may arise, such as language barriers, misunderstandings or cultural differences. Of course the unexpected may occur, but by dealing decisively with issues however infrequent, means you always have a plan to adapt as necessary. Try to offer practical solutions and strategies to address these challenges when they occur. For guest health and financial emergencies, the school is their first point of contact. A good school will always have 'Plan B' ready.

Effective Communication with Your Guest

Effective communication is essential for a successful hosting experience. Explore various communication tools and resources, such as translation apps like Google Translate, to bridge language gaps between you and your guest. Translation apps sometimes provide inaccurate translations and should really be used as a last resort. It is always in the best interests of your guest for them to really try hard to convey their message in spoken English and avoid apps.

Dealing with Homesickness or Culture Shock

Homesickness and culture shock can affect your guest's emotional well-being. Empathy goes a long way to helping the guest in these circumstances. Encourage them to stay connected with their family and seeking support from their fellow colleagues at school and the school staff when needed.

Incompatibility Between Hosts and Guests

Sometimes, personality clashes or incompatibilities may arise between hosts and guests. Encourage open communication to find mutually agreeable solutions. Explain clearly and immediately what issues you have and ask for their impressions and solutions.

If they prove more difficult, then speak with your contact at the school for advice. Most schools have a change clause so that if issues cannot be resolved, then either party can request a change of host or guest within one week. It is a rare occurrence, but it does happen, so stay calm and professional during all discussions.

Over the course of 10 years of hosting, this has only happened to us on two occasions and was swiftly and comfortably resolved for the guest and ourselves.

Differing Personal Hygiene Practices

Not every nationality in the world has the same hygiene practices. That doesn't mean they are dirty or smelly, just a different approach. So be open to accommodating different practices that your guest may have, and ensure they have access to the necessary facilities and supplies.

Feminine Hygiene

Provide information on the disposal of feminine hygiene products in your home and make sure your guest is aware of where to purchase them if needed. Sensitivity and privacy are essential when discussing such topics.

Extending Their Stay Due to Unexpected Circumstances

Address the possibility of unexpected circumstances, such as lockdowns, visa issues, travel restrictions or cancelled flights, that may require your guest to extend their stay.

Discuss how such situations will be managed, including housing arrangements and communication with your language school or agency.

You need to hear such possibilities from the guest themselves and from the school's accommodation officer, in case this causes a date clash with your next guest arrival.

Again this is a rare event, but an extra day or week of hosting is usually only beneficial to your financial account.

During the pandemic lockdown we had a lady from South Korea and a gentleman from Japan. Neither could get back home as they had originally planned, so we had them here for Christmas, which was great fun and an eye-opener for them with roast turkey and all the trimmings, plus Christmas pud, let alone hats in crackers and table games!

As part of the festivities we asked them to come up with typical table games from their own culture and great fun was had all round.

CHAPTER 14: The End of the Hosting Period

As the hosting period comes to a close, it's essential to navigate this transition thoughtfully and ensure a positive experience. If you are taking a break between your first guest and your next, it helps to have a family meeting and discuss positive and negative aspects of your hosting experience and to formulate ideas to make the next experience easier for all parties involved. In this chapter, we will explore the various aspects of concluding the hosting period.

Preparing for the End of the Hosting Period

In the days leading up to your guest's departure, take steps to prepare for their exit. This includes reviewing any remaining logistical details, ensuring they have all their belongings in order, maybe supplying an extra cardboard box if they have over-bought gifts or clothing to take home, along with a roll of strong packing tape and addressing any final questions or concerns.

One couple from Brazil who stayed three months with us, arrived with one large suitcase each, but left with five large suitcases between them, and even then they had to leave a few books behind due to lack of flight weight allowance! We have a cheap electronic suitcase weighing device (thanks Amazon) that we lend to the guest to check their suitcases the evening before departure.

For long-term guests, we have had several who have boxed up and posted some possessions home, which has cost them considerably less than buying an extra suitcase and the added cost of extra flight baggage. For example one guest from Japan sent a 12kg box home which cost her £66.00 (correct at date of book publication) from our local post office. Some extra documentation was required and you can help them fill-in the forms correctly.

On the day, make sure that they, and you also, have checked under the bed, down the back of the chairs and always right at the back of the drawers in their room for any wallets, passports, ID cards, family gifts, etc. that may have been missed during their packing. No one wants the stress of getting to the airport for their flight home and finding their travel documents are still in the bedroom in your house! Think of it as if it is you, about to leave your house for a foreign holiday trip.

Ask your guest to write a few words in a Guest Book, about their experience of hosting with you. This will pay off for you in spades, as you can use positive testimonials to boost your reputation as a gold-standard host family, and any negative points received to analyse and adjust, ready for your next guest.

It is common practice for schools to ask students to give feedback on their hosting experience, but the school doesn't always pass comments on to the hosts. Make sure to ask the school for the feedback after each guest has left.

Saying Goodbye and Staying in Touch

Saying goodbye can be emotional if you find you have bonded with your guest, but it's an essential part of the hosting experience. Share your gratitude and reflections on the time spent together, exchange contact information and discuss how you'll stay in touch. Some guests you genuinely gel with and form a lasting friendship. Try to maintain contact with your guests through emails, social media, or occasional visits if possible. These connections can last a lifetime and can make for great holiday adventures with a ready and willing tour guide!.

Lastly, take a selfie photo with the departing guest and note their name and dates they stayed with you, as a reminder for you both of shared memories. Having hosted 15+ guests per year, it is not easy remembering each one without the photo and details.

Preparing for Your Next Guest

If you plan to host another guest after the current one departs, prepare your home and yourself for the new arrival.

Ensure that the guest room is dusted, vacuumed and ready with fresh bedding, towels, etc., the bathroom is clean and clear of any shampoos, soaps lotions, make-up and medicines left by the previous guest. Check electrical cables to extension sockets, bedside lights and any other appliances for wear and tear, and mend them if required.

Again, a written checklist to tick off items as they are done, can be useful for you.

Review any specific preferences or requirements with your hosting agency or school, and be open to adapting your hosting approach based on the new guest's needs and goals.

We regularly have guests back-to-back, so that when one leaves, usually on a Sunday morning, we then have another arriving in four hours or so, and for this we must be ready with a fast and deep room clean, accessories replacement and appropriate food in stock.

Reflecting on Your Hosting Experience

So how was your first experience of hosting? Did you enjoy it? Did you make a good profit? Was it hard work for you and if so, why was that? Take the time to reflect on your hosting experience with all your family members that have taken part. Consider the moments of cultural exchange, personal growth and the connections forged with your guest. Reflect on the challenges you faced and the solutions you found, as well as the rewarding aspects of hosting.

Don't forget that there is a vast amount of useful resources available to assist you, not only from the schools themselves but also through websites that we cover in the following chapter, plus access to a Chat Forum so that you can ask questions and receive answers from many more experienced hosts. One day soon, you will be the ones answering the questions with knowledge and confidence, as you have become "Gold Standard Hosts".

CHAPTER 15: Resources and Additional Tips

First and Foremost

As part of this book, we offer you our hosting advice website: "Ultimate Hosting - How to Host International Guests as a Successful Business" at *https://www.ultimatehosting.me.uk*, where you can download an MS Word document of our 'House Rules' and alter them to suit your own information.

Plus links to UK Government and private websites that show you how to obtain a DBS check, legal obligations, tax information, medical help for guests and many other relevant topics. This includes a Chat Forum to ask questions and get swift replies from us and your fellow hosts, plus access to a free monthly newsletter 'The International Host's Chronicle - your monthly guide to hosting excellence'.

We also ask you to leave feedback on this book. Did we miss any vital aspects that you wish you had known before starting to host, or that you have learnt over the years?. Please let us know and we will review your comments to include in a second edition, with attribution. Any comments that lead to changes will receive a free copy of the second edition on publication, so please don't forget to leave your contact details.

Other Useful Websites and Organisations

Explore a list of websites and organisations that can offer guidance, information and support throughout your hosting experience.

This list is correct on first publication - November 2023 and probably won't change, however; updates can be found on our website: Ultimate Hosting at https://www.ultimatehosting.me.uk, through our free monthly newsletter: "The International Host's Chronicle", and with more urgent updates such as important regulation changes and new resources by occasional emails direct to you.

We have a personal dislike of newsletters and emails that bombard our inbox every day, so we promise if you register on the website, we will only send out the newsletters once per month and will keep emails to an absolute minimum.

ENGLISH UK is the national association of English language centres in the UK:
https://www.englishuk.com/en/about-us

Cambridge - English language free learning resources:
https://www.cambridgeenglish.org/learning-english/free-resources/

HMRC Property Income Manual:
https://www.gov.uk/hmrc-internal-manuals/property-income-manual/pim4001

Basic DBS checks:
https://www.gov.uk/guidance/basic-dbs-checks-guidance

When to use NHS 111 online or call 111:
https://www.nhs.uk/nhs-services/urgent-and-emergency-care-services/when-to-use-111/

ACKNOWLEDGEMENTS

My grateful thanks to Nic Dodgson for her tireless devotion as a host-mother, to Jan D'Amato in Naples, Italy for proof reading and editing the book, to Ali Passmore of ELC Brighton, with whom we have worked for the last 10 years and who has kindly written the Foreword, to all the lovely guests we have had the great pleasure to host over the years, and for those many guests yet to come.

Front cover image courtesy of Duy Pham via Unsplash.
https://unsplash.com/@duy-pham

LEGAL DISCLAIMER

The contents of this book are provided "as-is" without any express or implied warranties, representations, or guarantees of any kind, including but not limited to fitness for a particular purpose, merchantability, accuracy, completeness, or reliability.

The author and publisher expressly disclaim any and all liability for any direct, indirect, consequential, incidental, or special damages that may arise from the use or inability to use the information or materials contained in this book, regardless of whether such damages result from contractual or extra-contractual claims.

The information and materials presented in this book are intended for general informational purposes only and should not be considered as professional or expert advice. The reader should use their own judgement and discretion when applying the information from this book to specific situations.

The author and publisher do not warrant or represent that the information contained in this book is error-free, up-to-date, or suitable for any particular purpose. The reader assumes full responsibility for any risks or consequences that may arise from the use of the information contained herein.

This disclaimer is a binding part of the terms of use of this book. By reading, using, or accessing the contents of this book, you agree to the terms and conditions outlined in this disclaimer. If you do not agree with these terms, you should refrain from using or relying on the information provided in this book.

This disclaimer is subject to change without notice. It is the responsibility of the reader to review this disclaimer periodically for any updates or modifications.

Printed in Great Britain
by Amazon